Dallas Today

Robert A. Lawrence

Taylor Publishing Company
Dallas, Texas

Copyright © 1985, Taylor Publishing Company,
1550 West Mockingbird Lane, Dallas, Texas 75235

Library of Congress Cataloging in Publication Data

Lawrence, Robert, 1948—
  Dallas today

  Includes index.
  1. Dallas (Tex.) — Description.   I. Title.
F394.D214L38   1985   976.4′ 2812063   85-4649
ISBN 0-87833-483-1

Printed in the United States of America

Acknowledgements

During the year of research, writing, and photography devoted to this book, I was assisted by several individuals who deserve special recognition. At the outset, I sought the advice of Cathey Peat, one of the city's best independent production coordinators, who familiarized me with the many technical and procedural aspects of color reproduction and printing. I also benefited from the expertise of Nancy Meyer, who briefed me on the fundamentals of typography.

I am particularly grateful to Sherrie Brenn who contributed several of the photographs in this book, and assisted me on numerous occasions. I am also indebted to Deborah Thiessen, an exceptionally-talented hairstylist and makeup artist who I frequently call on to put the "glamour" in my glamour photography.

Perhaps the most challenging task I faced was the accumulation of more than 100 color photographs that would adequately depict the extraordinary appearance and atmosphere that is unique to "Big D". I determined early on that a great deal of new photography would be required, and as it turned out, 80% of the photos included were taken specifically for *Dallas Today*.

As the photo credits will reveal, I took most of these photographs myself. Though I have pursued my interest in photography for more than 20 years, first as an amateur and later as a professional, my style and technique benefited most from the few months I shared my studio with Jean Meziere. This internationally-published master photographer's encouragement had a great deal to do with my decision to undertake this project, and the time I spent with him before his return to Paris was an invaluable experience.

Since *Dallas Today* is to be followed by a continuing series of pictorial essays on the world's great cities, I was determined to produce an impressive high-quality product. My confidence was greatly enhanced when the enormous resources of Taylor Publishing Company became involved.

And finally, I must express my deepest appreciation for the civic-minded Dallasites who provided the financial support that enabled me to devote a year of my time to this project: Tony Kaufmann, Roger Cramer, Dave Tapley, Ellen Humphreys, Judy Connor, Donald Guinn, Sherrie Brenn, Jeff Cramblit, and Jerry Harkins.

Robert A. Lawrence
March, 1985

Contents

An Introduction to Dallas

Sports, Entertainment, The Arts

Education, Religion, Health

Shopping in Dallas

First Class Hotels

Epilogue

An Introduction to Dallas

As you will discover in reading the narrative that accompanies this pictorial essay, describing the most impressive aspects of the City of Dallas is an exercise in superlatives. Dallas is truly a remarkable city, and its citizens are prone to display a large degree of the sort of grandiose pride that Texans in general are famous for. Nevertheless, as a native of the rival state across the Red River, I can claim sufficient objectivity to insist that there is no subtle way to adequately describe this city.

I must also emphasize that *Dallas Today* has been published primarily for your enjoyment, and though I have attempted to provide accurate and up-to-date information, the facts and figures you will read are based solely on my personal observations and the data that was available to me at the time. Dallas is growing so rapidly that the passage of a few months can alter statistical data appreciably, but one fact remains unchanged month after month and year after year: Dallas is an extraordinary city that continues to benefit from generation after generation of outstanding leadership and uncommon civic pride.

The **WESTERN SKYLINE** pictured above is seen from across the Trinity River channel. For many years Dallas visionaries have proposed the creation of a beautiful recreational lake on this site. This exciting development will surely bring new life and even greater economic growth to downtown Dallas, and Dallas tradition dictates that it's only a matter of time until "Town Lake" becomes a reality.

Dallas history began in 1841 when a Tennessee lawyer and trader named John Neely Bryan established a trading post on the east bank of the Trinity River near present-day downtown Dallas. His small log cabin, the first house erected in Dallas, is on display at **FOUNDERS PLAZA.**

Nearby, in dramatic contrast, are both the old and new Dallas County Courthouses. The cube-shaped structure in front of the new courthouse is a memorial to President John F. Kennedy.

Dallas' proud heritage of outstanding civic leadership dates all the way back to its beginnings. Having won the battle for the county seat in 1846 when the city was only five years old, the resourcefulness of its townspeople was challenged again when it was learned that the nation's first railroads intended to bypass this seemingly unimportant settlement on the banks of the Trinity River. A well-orchestrated campaign to change the minds of key railroad officials resulted in the arrival of Dallas' first rail line in 1874.

Subsequent generations have carried on this tradition of aggressive leadership which has led to the city's emergence as the Southwest's leading distribution center. The city is now served by a massive transportation network that includes the world's largest airport, 42 commercial airlines, 112 cargo carriers, 80 charter airlines, more than 50 major trucking firms, 8 railroads, 5 bus lines, and 25 major highways including 7 spokes of the Interstate Highway system.

In the midst of Dallas' unparalleled growth and progress, there are a number of civic and private organizations dedicated to the preservation of the city's rich and colorful heritage.

The completely restored *Wilson House* on **SWISS AVENUE** in east Dallas is a rare and beautiful example of the many magnificent Victorian mansions that were built in Dallas around the turn of the century. In 1977, Dallas' leading homebuilder, Dave Fox, purchased the five decaying homes in the 2900 block of Swiss Avenue, known as the "Wilson Block", with the intent of saving the historically-significant neighborhood from inevitable destruction and redevelopment. He enlisted the aid of the *Historic Preservation League* to develop a plan for the restoration and effective use of the Wilson block.

In 1980, the *Meadows Foundation,* a philanthropic organization founded in 1948 by Texas oil magnate, Algur H. Meadows, purchased the properties and funded the complete restoration of the Wilson Block. The block now houses a unique consortium of non-profit community service organizations including the Meadows Foundation, the Historic Preservation League, and the Greater Dallas Council of Churches.

The *Dallas County Heritage Society* was formed in 1966 for the purpose of preserving Dallas' architectural heritage. With the cooperation of the *Dallas Park and Recreation Department,* the city's oldest park, dedicated in 1876, was selected as an appropriate site for the relocation and restoration of many historically-significant structures that trace Dallas' architectural history from the city's beginnings to the early twentieth century. The first structure to be moved to what is now called **OLD CITY PARK** was Millermore, the largest remaining antebellum home in Dallas.

Pictured here is the beautifully-restored George House, c. 1901, which is one of more than two dozen authentic 19th

century structures located in this fascinating microcosm of Dallas history. Other buildings include a railroad depot, doctor's office, general store, bank, hotel, church, school, and road house, all of which are arranged in a manner reminiscent of a 19th century township.

Historic preservation has also become an important priority in the downtown area. One of Dallas' earliest landmarks, the Magnolia Building with Mobil's neon Pegasus perched on its rooftop, the Adolphus Hotel, the Majestic Theatre, and the Union Terminal, are among the historic buildings that have been renovated and saved for future generations.

MODERN DOWNTOWN DALLAS is the heart of the thriving and rapidly-expanding Metroplex. More than 62,000 business establishments and about 5,000 manufacturing companies are located in Dallas County. The Metroplex has a labor force of almost two million, and one of the nation's lowest unemployment rates.

The Dallas/Ft. Worth Standard Metropolitan Statistical Area, commonly referred to as the "Metroplex", is the largest SMSA in Texas and the eighth largest in the United States with a total area of 8,360 square miles, and a population of more than 3.2 million.

The focus of this book, however, is generaly limited to the boundaries of Dallas County which has a land area of 859 square miles, and a population in excess of 1.6 million of which about 1 million live within the city limits of Dallas.

The topography is relatively flat, ranging from 450' to 750' above sea level. Hot summers and mild winters result in an average yearly temperature of 65.7 degrees. Average rainfall is 40.75 inches, and Dallas air is among the cleanest found in a major U.S. city.

Compared to other major cities, the cost of living in Dallas is also favorable. For example, if your annual living expenses in Dallas are about $30,000, the same standard of living would cost you $34,000 in Los Angeles, or $42,000 in New York. There is no personal or corporate income tax at the state or local level, and Dallas property taxes are below the average for major metropolitan areas.

Just how fast is downtown Dallas growing? In 1983 Dallas led the nation in construction and real estate activity. $1.8 billion in commerical real estate loans were recorded, and Dallas' **CENTRAL BUSINESS DISTRICT** was expanded by 5 million square feet of new office space!

Downtown's total office space has risen to more than 37 million square feet with approximately 2.5 million of that completed in 1984 alone. By 1987, it is projected that the central business district will contain a whopping 45 million square feet of office space!

At this writing there are more than 90 construction projects underway in downtown Dallas, and it is interesting to note that two of Dallas' largest construction companies, Austin Industries and HCB Contractors, together account for 50% of all high-rise construction in downtown Dallas.

Although about a third of Dallas' new office space is absorbed by companies relocating to the Dallas area, the majority of it is occupied by prosperous and rapidly-growing Dallas business firms — another positive indication of the city's excellent business climate and favorable economic conditions.

Eighteen publicly-held non-financial corporations headquartered in the Metroplex had revenues in excess of one billion dollars in 1983, with Southland Corporation leading the way with $8.8 billion in revenues.

Dun & Bradstreet's "Million Dollar Directory" lists more than 1100 Metroplex-based companies with assets greater than one million dollars, ranking Dallas third behind New York and Chicago.

Dallas' incredible growth rate is not limited to office space alone. In 1983, 4.8 million square feet of retail lease space was added, bringing the city's total leasable retail space to 56.8 million square feet! This figure is particularly impressive in that it includes no new major shopping centers which normally account for a large portion of the new space added in recent record-breaking years.

Ten major retail department store chains operate 60 stores in Dallas. The largest, Sanger Harris, occupies two million square feet with its 13 stores. Other leaders include Dillard's with 11 stores occupying 1.8 million square feet, Joske's with 8 stores occupying 1.6 million square feet, and Neiman-Marcus with 4 stores occupying 800,000 square feet.

Metroplex retail space will increase by 7.3 million square feet in 1984 bringing the total up to an incredible 84.8 million square feet.

Dallas is indeed a model of free enterprise at its very best. During the past year almost 50,000 people have moved to Dallas to take advantage of the abundant opportunities to be found here. These newcomers, as well as thousands of longtime Dallasites, will find Dallas' many outstanding attributes, such as the beautiful view of **DOWNTOWN BY NIGHT,** an inspiration to their personal and professional growth.

Dallas' council-manager form of municipal government has been an important factor in the city's long history of progress and prosperity. The mayor heads a ten member elected city council which functions like a corporate board of directors in determining policy and charting the city's future course.

The council employs a professional city manager who is responsible for the daily operation of all city departments and services in much the same manner as a corporate president operates his company. Candidates for the council are not identified by political party affiliation during the campaign process. The resulting reduction in partisan politics permits council members to vote in accordance with their perception of the city's needs and other practical considerations rather than party loyalties.

The city's operating budget for fiscal 84-85 is $1.14 billion of which $3.6 million is dedicated to the support and advancement of the arts.

Dallas' unique **CITY HALL** was designed by famous architect I.M. Pei, and dedicated in March of 1978. The striking cantilevered design, 122' high and 560' long, was the subject of much controversy during the planning stages; but it is now a source of great pride to Dallasites old and new.

A beautifully-landscaped promenade with a large fountain pool separates City Hall from the impressive new Dallas Public Library directly across the street.

Numerous factors have contributed to the city's phenomenal growth. Dallas' selection as the home of the 11th District Federal Reserve Bank led to the development of what is now the 5th largest banking center in the U.S.; and the city ranks second nationally in the number of insurance company headquarters.

Dallas' continuously-expanding convention and trade show facilities have placed it among the nation's top three convention sites, and the State Fair of Texas has become the largest annual exposition of its kind.

Dallas has spawned countless self-made millionaires, and it is second only to New York City in the number of residents who appeared on the *Forbes Magazine* 1984 list of America's richest people. As a matter of fact, of the twelve individuals in the United States who are reported to be worth more than $1 billion, five are Dallasites.

SAN JACINTO TOWER, pictured here, along with the adjacent Bryan Tower, are included among the estimated $6.5 billion in real estate holdings controlled by Trammell Crow and his partners. Crow is now considered the largest private real estate developer in the nation, and in 1983 alone was responsible for $1.5 billion in construction starts. Crow, who began his professional career as a bank teller, and later became a CPA, launched his enormous real estate empire with the construction of a small warehouse in 1948.

16

Dallas' long history of prosperity and economic growth has been fueled by a strong banking industry which is now ranked as the nation's fifth largest. There are now more than 150 banks in Dallas, including the 11th District Federal Reserve Bank.

The magnificent 70-story InterFirst Plaza building pictured above is now the tallest building in Dallas, rising 921 feet above street level. This ambitious real estate development, which features extraordinary and innovative interior design, is the creation of InterFirst Bank, Dallas; Bramalea, Ltd.; and PIC Realty Corporation.

InterFirst Plaza headquarters the InterFirst Corporation, which, as of the second quarter of 1984, is the largest bank holding company in the state of Texas. InterFirst Bank, Dallas, is the lead bank in a statewide chain of 65 banks which claim total assets in excess of $20 billion.

DALLAS BANKS are particularly fond of real estate transactions. In 1983 alone, Dallas banks recorded more than $1.8 billion in commercial real estate loans! Indeed, those with impressive financial statements and solid cash-flow will find dozens of eager Dallas bankers ready to fund a variety of worthwhile business ventures.

THANKSGIVING SQUARE is symbolic of the Dallas business community's committment to character and integrity in the pursuit of prosperity. This beautiful plaza in the heart of downtown Dallas offers a comfortable and inspiring environment where downtowners may relax and meditate amidst the fast-paced atmosphere of the central business district.

Indeed, downtown Dallas embodies the spirit and the legacy of the great leaders who have created it. Names like Stemmons, Thornton, Rodgers, Meadows, Hoblitzelle, and Dealey provide continuing inspiration for today's leaders who are faced with even greater responsibilities and greater challenges.

One such leader is Ross Perot, who has consistently displayed his willingness to spare no effort or expense in the continuing quest to improve the quality of life in this city. Perot launched his computer services firm, Electronic Data Systems, in 1962 with $1000 of his own money. By 1970 his company was worth more than a billion dollars. The true test of character came when a disastrous stock market plunge resulted in a loss of $1 billion over a thirty-day period! What did this incredible man do? He picked up the pieces and rebuilt his fortune. In 1984 he sold EDS to General Motors for a reported $2.5 billion.

Perot is now leading a statewide campaign for educational reform with the intention of creating the nation's finest public school system for future generations of Texans.

THANKSGIVING TOWER,
adjacent to Thanksgiving Square,
headquarters the business
interests of Dallas' wealthiest and
most influencial family. Perhaps
only television's mythical Ewing
family is more famous than the
family of oil billionaire H.L.
Hunt. The Hunt legacy began
when H.L. played a hunch and
bought the mineral rights to some
obscure East Texas farmland with
borrowed money. $100 million
worth of oil production provide
the Hunt family with a nice
bankroll that his ten children
have parlayed into a $10 billion
empire.

Four of the Hunt children are
billionaires according to *Forbes
Magazine:* Bunker Hunt holds 5
million acres of real estate
worldwide in addition to his
share of the family's oil business,
and his sister Caroline has
invested more than $250 million
in luxury hotels in Dallas,
Houston, and Beverly Hills.

Herbert Hunt is principal
member of the family's vast oil
empire; and Margaret, H.L.'s
eldest heir, is regarded as the
family matriarch since the death
of her father.

Lamar Hunt is the sportsman of
the family. He co-founded the
American Football League, owns
the Kansas City Chiefs, and now
devotes most of his time to World
Championship Tennis, Inc.

H.L. Hunt's second family,
consisting of his second wife and
four more children, inherited
$250 million from their father.
Under the management of Ray
Hunt, the second family's fortune
is now estimated at $1 billion.

Ray Hunt is also primarily responsible for Dallas' most recognizable landmark. When the plans were unveiled for Reunion Center which would include a fabulous new Hyatt Regency Hotel, the adjacent 50-story Reunion Tower with the big ball on top was the subject of controversy among Dallas' more conservative forces. But once again progress and imagination prevailed and the Reunion Tower is now the focal point of the rapidly-expanding Dallas skyline.

Nearby **REUNION ARENA** is a state-of-the-art sports and entertainment facility which is owned by the City of Dallas. Reunion Arena is the home of the Dallas Mavericks, and the site of many other sports events, concerts, and conventions.

This 18,000 seat air-conditioned arena was completed in 1980 at a cost of $27 million dollars and has since attracted numerous concert performances by the entertainment industry's biggest stars, including Frank Sinatra who holds the arena record of $300,000 in ticket sales for a single performance.

The old warehouse and commercial district on the west side of downtown Dallas was officially designated as **THE WEST END HISTORIC DISTRICT** in 1975. This action came as the result of the efforts of several influential Dallas citizens who wanted to save the last remnants of early 20th century Dallas from the bulldozers of redevelopment. The plan called for renovation of more than 20 historic structures which would be occupied by unique restaurants, retail shops, office space, and even residential housing. City bond elections provided funds for landscaping and street improvements and the developers finally moved in when the federal government offered up to a 25% investment tax credit for the preservation and renovation of historic buildings. A year later the city added the additional incentive of an eight year tax freeze at pre-improvement evaluations for those who renovate downtown historic buildings.

These multi-million dollar renovation projects are providing many businesses with an affordable but nonetheless luxurious alternative to the high-rise steel and glass lease space of the central business district.

The brick building in the lower left corner of the photo is the Texas Schoolbook Depository building from which Lee Harvey Oswald shot President John F. Kennedy in 1963. Even though the leadership and citizens of Dallas had given JFK a warm welcome, and in spite of the fact that Oswald was an outsider, Dallas struggled for many years to overcome the stigma of that infamous event.

On June 7, 1936, President Franklin D. Roosevelt presided over the opening ceremonies of the Texas Centennial Exposition. More than $25 million had been expended in the construction of several major structures and acres of elaborate landscaping. The six-month celebration that followed was attended by more than 6 million people!

Now known as *Fair Park,* this 277-acre complex has been continuously modernized and expanded over the years, and it now includes the 72,000 seat **COTTON BOWL** stadium, the 3,400 seat Music Hall, a 7,200 seat coliseum, a 4,000 seat open-air Band Shell, six major exhibit buildings, livestock facilities, a permanent Midway amusement park, and six museums including the *Museum of Natural History,* the *Texas Hall of State,* the *Dallas Garden Center,* the *Dallas Aquarium, The Science Place,* and the *Age of Steam Museum.*

Fair Park hosts the annual Texas State Fair, the largest of its kind in the United States. The state fair draws an attendance of approximately 3 million visitors each year during its 17-day run, and as many as 355,000 persons have passed through the gates in a single day.

The Cotton Bowl stadium is the sight of numerous sports and entertainment events including the annual New Year's Day Cotton Bowl Classic, the annual Texas-OU football game, and the Texas World Music Festival which drew a record crowd of 82,251 persons in 1979.

Work is presently underway on a multi-million dollar renovation and expansion program in preparation for the Texas Sesquicentennial Exposition in 1986.

The Dallas Chamber of Commerce reports that 2 million persons will come to Dallas during the coming year for the purpose of attending one of the 2,000 conventions, markets, and trade shows scheduled here.

The outstanding facilities of the **DALLAS CONVENTION CENTER** have been a major factor in establishing Dallas as the nation's third most popular location for convention and trade show activities. This world-class facility encompasses almost 1 million square feet including Memorial Auditorium, the site of frequent sports, civic, and entertainment events.

The city's excellent convention facilities are supported by more than 32,000 first-class hotel rooms. Many of Dallas' finest hotels are featured elsewhere in this book.

The Dallas Convention Center was the site of the 1984 Republican National Convention which provides another prime example of Dallas' superior leadership. In contrast to the estimated $8 million in public funds expended by San Francisco to defray expenses in connection with the 1984 Democratic National Convention, Dallasites Bill Cooper and Trammell Crow raised the $4 million required for the Republican Convention from their business associates in the private sector. Not a cent of taxpayers' money was spent.

More than 20 years ago, a visionary Dallas real estate developer was among the first to foresee Dallas as a city of great international stature. He conceived a plan that would eventually establish Dallas as a major center of international trade.

Trammell Crow's *Dallas Market Center* is now the world's largest wholesale merchandise mart. A few minutes north of downtown on Interstate 35, this sprawling 150-acre complex includes the World Trade Center, the Apparel Mart, the Menswear Mart, the Trade Mart, Market Hall, the Homefurnishings Mart, and the new Infomart. Excluding the Infomart which is presently nearing completion, the Dallas Market Center provides 8 million square feet of display area.

More than 500,000 buyers from throughout the U.S. and 35 foreign nations purchase $6 billion worth of merchandise annually from the thousands of manufacturers and wholesale distributors who maintain showrooms in the Dallas Market Center.

The fabulous **APPAREL MART**'s 1.8 million square feet houses 2,000 showrooms, and as you might expect, is the world's largest fashion merchandising mart. The new Menswear Mart adds an additional 400,000 square feet expandable to 1.7 million square feet.

These Dallas Market Center facilities have established Dallas as one of the nation's three principle fashion markets, and have played a vital role in creating the city's fashionable image.

The Apparel Mart is the focal point of the Dallas fashion industry, and located on the ground floor is the internationally-recognized *Kim Dawson Agency*. The Dawson Agency is the largest and best-known modeling agency between New York and Los Angeles, and each year it attracts legions of young hopefuls in pursuit of a modeling career.

The beautiful and stylish appearance of the fashion models seen in television commercials and magazine ads is cultivated through months and often years of training and experience under the expert guidance of top agents like Kim Dawson and Mike Beaty.

Provided one meets basic physical qualifications, becoming a successful model involves a great deal of hard work and unrelenting determination. Futhermore, without the services of talented makeup artists and hairstylists, the typical model would be indistinguishable from the many attractive people one encounters on a normal day about town.

The competitive beauty-oriented environment created by a thriving modeling industry in a fashion-conscious city contributes a great deal toward Dallas' reputation as one of the great glamour capitals of the world.

Dallas women take pride in their appearance as well as their achievements. This composite photo is but a small sampling of **DALLAS GLAMOUR.**

THE WORLD TRADE CENTER is another magnificent monument to free enterprise. Manufacturers and distributors from all over the world display their wares for the benefit of thousands of buyers from every corner of the U.S. as well as many foreign countries. This giant center of international trade is a fundamental factor in Dallas' emergence as a world-class city.

Nearby, the newest element of the Dallas Market Center is nearing completion. The Infomart (International Information Processing Market Center) is patterned after London's famed Crystal Palace of 1851. This $92 million facility will be a permanent display, demonstration, and training center for the international computer industry.

Such industry giants as Texas Instruments, AT&T, Xerox, and IBM will be among the hundreds of computer industry manufacturers and distributors which will occupy this 7-story 1.5 million square foot building.

Dallas is now the 5th largest computer market in the U.S., and by 1986 the city is expected to rank third in the number of installed computer bases.

Dallas has long been recognized as a leader in the development and marketing of computer technology and related high-tech products, and the Infomart should greatly enhance the growth and prosperity of high-tech industry in the Metroplex.

THE CRESCENT is a uniquely-designed mixed-use development that will provide 1.25 million square feet of luxury office space in three towers, a 25-room Crescent Court Hotel, and a three-level open courtyard featuring dozens of unique specialty shops and retail merchants. The huge excavation pictured above, the largest ever dug in Dallas, will accomodate a 4,100-car underground parking garage.

The Crescent is located just north of downtown in the Oak Lawn area. This historically-significant residential and commercial community has been the site of extensive redevelopment and restoration activity during the past few years.

Oak Lawn offers a more relaxed picturesque atmosphere in contrast to the fast-paced futuristic atmosphere that prevails in nearby downtown Dallas. A large portion of the city's advertising and creative arts community lives and works in Oak Lawn, having been lured to the Dallas area by the extraordinary growth of advertising industry which is now ranked third nationally.

Although there are more than 300 advertising agencies in Dallas, three major firms dominate the market. The largest of these, Bozell & Jacobs, employs more than 350 persons to handle more than $250 million in accounts. Tracey-Locke/BBDO and the Bloom agency account for another $250-300 million in annual billings, and together with scores of smaller agencies, these firms have brought rapidly-increasing national recognition to the Dallas advertising industry.

In contrast with the concrete, steel, and glass of the central business district, Dallas includes numerous locales where greenbelts, woodlands, and rolling hills dominate the landscape.

Pictured here is a view of **LAKESIDE PARK,** a beautiful creekside park located in the exclusive Highland Park community north of downtown Dallas. Many of the Dallas area's largest and most beautiful residences can be found in Highland Park, which is actually a separately incorporated city located entirely within the boundaries of the city of Dallas.

There are many other exceptionally beautiful areas within the city, including portions of Oak Cliff, East Dallas, North Dallas, and the White Rock Lake area where the magnificent Hunt family mansion is located.

Perhaps the most important development in the Dallas residential housing market at present is a growing interest in the construction of new, quality housing in the downtown area. Dallas homebuilder, Dave Fox, has provided aggressive leadership in providing the inner-city residential development that is vital to the campaign to bring life to downtown Dallas.

His firm, Fox & Jacobs, has built more than 45,000 homes in the Metroplex, and the company's exciting Bryan Place development on the eastern edge of downtown Dallas is bringing many executives and young professionals to the downtown area.

EXALL PARK, pictured above, is the centerpiece of the Bryan Place development, and is characteristic of several beautiful greenbelts in or near the downtown area.

Plans are currently underway for residential construction in the West End Historic District and along Woodall Rodgers Freeway which borders downtown to the north.

Those who are interested in up-to-date information about quality-built affordable housing in the Dallas-area will find an abundance of useful information in *Dallas Today Magazine.*

LUXURY HOMES are abundant in Dallas for those who have the means to enjoy the very best in custom-built homes. This beautiful north Dallas home is but one example of thousands of richly-appointed custom homes to be found throughout Dallas.

In 1983, Dallas led the nation in both single-family and multi-family residential construction; and during the first half of 1984, 30,780 multi-family permits, and 18,000 single-family permits were issued.

As the Dallas economy grows, so does the purchasing power of its citizens, and the current record-breaking trends in the housing market are both another indication of the phenomenal growth and prosperity of the City of Dallas.

Luxury Homes Magazine is a popular source of information for discriminating homebuyers who are looking for the finest residential properties that Dallas has to offer.

Ben C. Carpenter grew up on the sprawling Hackberry Creek Ranch that his father, John Carpenter, had purchased in 1928. By the late 1960s, Ben realized that this choice real estate, ideally situated between downtown Dallas and what would soon become the world's largest airport, would inevitably be consumed by commercial expansion. He was determined that it be developed in a manner that would preserve the natural beauty of the land.

In September of 1973, Ben Carpenter and Dan Williams of Southland Corporation unveiled an ambitious master plan for a beautiful 12,000-acre commercial and residential development. **LAS COLINAS** would, in just ten years, become one of the nation's most prestigious business addresses.

More than 400 companies have located in Las Colinas, including such international giants as IBM, General Motors, Xerox, AT&T, Sony, Panasonic, Rockwell International, DuPont, McDonnell Douglas, Texaco, Diamond Shamrock, and many others too numerous to mention.

IBM alone occupies nearly 1 million square feet of space, and the monumental new Williams Square complex adds another 1.7 million square feet to this phenomenally-successful development.

Residential development in Las Colinas is equally impressive. A wide range of quality housing for up to 50,000 people is an important feature of the master plan, and 4,000 acres are committed to parks, golf courses, recreation, and cultural facilties.

In January of 1974, **D/FW AIRPORT** opened its runways for the first time and began operations as the world's largest commercial airport facility. This ultra-modern 17,500-acre airport has since become the world's sixth busiest airport with more than 1,200 daily operations.

DFW's twelve original carriers have increased to more than 50 domestic and foreign airlines. An average of 600 daily departures provide service to 150 U.S. cities and 24 foreign ports. During its tenth year of operation, D/FW accommodated 26 million air travelers!

Even more remarkable is D/FW's tremendous capacity for expansion to meet the increasing transportation needs of the rapidly-developing Metroplex. The 90 boarding gates now in use can be expanded to 234, and proposed runway expansions will increase the airports total VFR capacity to 300 operations per hour.

By the year 2000, D/FW Airport will have the capacity to accommodate more than 150 million passengers annually, and it may well become the world's busiest airport. In addition to its vital role in stimulating the unprecedented growth of the Dallas area, D/FW provides employment for more than 20,000 people, and contributes $11 million per day to the Metroplex economy.

Appropriately located in the center of the world's largest airport is the world's largest airport hotel! The magnificent *Amfac Hotel* offers 1,450 deluxe rooms as well as excellent dining and entertainment.

Prior to the opening of D/FW airport in 1974, **LOVE FIELD** was the center of Dallas aviation. This 1,400-acre airfield was originally opened in 1917 as a U.S. Army aviation training center, and later purchased by the City of Dallas for general and commercial aviation in 1928.

By 1973, passenger traffic had reached an annual level of almost 7 million enplanements, making it the nation's 6th busiest airport, before it lost all but one of its carriers to the new airport in early 1974. Southwest Airlines maintained its operations at Love Field, and together with regional carrier Muse Air, which initiated service in 1981, enplanements have increased to almost 3 millions as of 1983.

General aviation, however, accounts for the majority of air traffic at Love Field now, with a total of 177,000 private aircraft operations recorded for 1983. Many of Dallas' top corporations and private business interests maintain aircraft at this convenient facility which is just 15 minutes from downtown Dallas.

The terminal baggage claim area is currently undergoing a $2 million renovation, and a $20 million, 4,000 space, parking garage is currently in the planning stages.

Sports,
Entertainment
& the Arts

The sixty-acre $2.6 billion Dallas Arts District project is the largest downtown development in the United States. In addition to providing Dallas with a world-class center for cultural education and the performing arts, this ambitious undertaking is calculated to spearhead a well-rooted campaign to give downtown Dallas another qualification in its bid to join the ranks of such cultural epicenters as New York, London, Paris, and San Francisco — a thriving inner-city population.

When civic leaders and developers are willing to provide downtown residency for sufficient numbers of executives, young professionals, and talented artists, they will breathe life into what is now a gargantuan single-purpose "facility", and downtown Dallas will assume a unique and identifiable character of its own.

The new **MUSEUM OF ART** is the cornerstone of the Arts District. This beautiful 210,000 square foot facility is a good example of the type of cooperation that gets things done in Dallas. In a 1979 bond election, the citizens of Dallas approved the largest allocation of public funds ($25 million) ever devoted to a cultural project in the U.S., for the construction of a new home for its Museum of Art. The business community responded with a matching $27 million in private funds, and Dallas gains a new world-class art museum.

THE MUSIC HALL, situated in Fair Park just east of downtown Dallas, was built in 1925 at a cost of $500,000. About fifty years later, this city-owned concert facility was renovated and expanded at a cost of $5.5 million. The comfort and elegance of this cavernous music hall is evidenced by virtually continuous use for symphony performances, operas, ballets, musicals, concerts, meetings, and rehearsals.

In addition to providing a home for the Dallas Symphony Orchestra for the past fifty years, the Music Hall also hosts Dallas' annual Summer Musicals program which brings to Dallas each summer the finest musical entertainment available this side of Broadway.

For more than 25 years, the Dallas Opera has staged its annual productions in the Music Hall, and for years, it was the only place in America where world-famous opera star, Maria Callas, would perform.

Though completion of the Dallas Symphony's new concert hall in the downtown arts district will temporarily relieve the Music Hall's crowded schedule of events, Dallas' emergence as an international cultural center will no doubt keep this historic facility filled with the sound of music for many years to come.

In May of 1900, five professional musicians and thirty-five musically-talented Dallas citizens performed for the first time under the direction of a German-born concert pianist. Thus, *Hans Kreissig*, who continued to direct this dedicated group of musicians for five years, is credited with founding the **DALLAS SYMPHONY ORCHESTRA.**

Forty years later, under the leadership of *Antal Dorati*, the DSO became an all-professional organization and began a steady climb to international prominence. Four more decades of outstanding musical talent and leadership has resulted in the emergence of one of the nation's finest orchestras.

Under the direction of internationally-acclaimed conductor Eduardo Mata since 1977, the DSO will soon occupy a new 213,000 square foot $50 million concert hall in the downtown Arts District.

The *Dallas Symphony Association* responds to its enthusiastic public support with an annual calendar of events that serves the entire population. Free *Concerts in the Park* make the symphony experience available to every family; and the lively *Superpops* series is a favorite among those who love the sound of their favorite popular tunes being performed by a world-class orchestra.

The classical series of concerts features a wide variety of world-famous guest conductors and performers, providing music lovers with an opportunity to see and hear the stirring performances of virtuoso talent from all nations.

Cultural development in Dallas has not been limited to art and music. When called upon to provide a first-class facility for the advancement of classical dance, business leaders and Dallas voters again joined forces to fund the complete restoration of downtown's magnificent Majestic Theatre at a cost of $5 million. In January of 1983, the sixty-year-old Majestic, a classic example of the opulent show houses of the early twentieth century, reopened its doors to provide a beautiful home for the **DALLAS BALLET.**

In 1981, the fully-professionalized Dallas Ballet Association appointed Danish-born Flemming Flindt to succeed the late George Skibine, the original artistic director of what was initially called the Dallas Civic Ballet Company.

Flemming Flindt's outstanding credits include a 12-year tenure as artistic director of the Royal Danish Ballet, a company with a heritage among ballet's richest. Under his direction, and with the type of public support that Dallas citizens are providing for the performing arts, the Dallas Ballet is rapidly rising to international prominence.

Sharing the newly-renovated Majestic with the Ballet is Nicola Resigno's **DALLAS OPERA.** Since its inaugural performance in 1957, featuring opera star Maria Callas, the Dallas Opera has received international acclaim for its splendid productions, its committment to the training of native talent, and its continuous efforts to stimulate public appreciation for this traditional art form through special student performances, workshops, and lectures throughout the Dallas area.

In 1959 **THE DALLAS THEATRE CENTER,** Dallas' original professional theater company, opened an exciting new facility — the only theater ever designed by eminent architect Frank Lloyd Wright. The DTC has since garnered numerous accolades on both the national and international level, and it has provided the foundation for a thriving legitimate theater community.

DTC's committment to excellence was further evidenced by the hiring of internationally-acclaimed artistic director, Adrian Hall, who has now opened a second DTC theater facility in the downtown arts district.

Several outstanding professional theater companies have now joined DTC in its efforts to provide Broadway-calibre theatrical performances for Dallas theater patrons.

Legendary humorist and philanthropist, Bob Hope, has long been the patron saint of the Dallas theater. His generous support has helped provide Southern Methodist University with one of the nation's finest collegiate drama departments; and his periodic personal appearances on the campus provide many promising performers with lifelong inspiration.

These thoroughly-trained, enthusiastic students of the theater will supply Dallas with a continuous source of exciting new talent for many generations to come.

So you've got a few million dollars, a great script, and you're looking for a place to make an academy award-winning motion picture? You'll need an enormous soundstage — about 15,000 square feet. And how about a state-of-the-art computerized lighting control system with 600 individual dimmers for 64 remote control lighting plaks suspended 34 feet above a 360° cyclorama?

Of course you'll also need first-class star dressing rooms, space for your hair and makeup people to work, production offices, rehearsal space, top quality sound recording facilities, and expert post-production services. Above all, you'll want a talented, experienced, and enthusiastic film crew that knows how to get the job done on schedule and under budget. And for the sake of credibility, make the film

in one of the nation's top three film production centers. Why not make it in Dallas at the new multi-million dollar **DALLAS COMMUNICATIONS COMPLEX?**

A few years ago, real estate developer Trammell Crow stepped forward in the tradition of Dallas' great leaders, and assumed responsibility for meeting the needs of what was then a small but enthusiatic and talented filmmaking community. He provided them with the largest and best-equipped film and video production facility this side of L.A.

In its first two years of operation, the Studios at Las Colinas have already generated an impressive array of film and television programming resulting in both Oscar and Emmy award nominations for local and visiting filmmakers.

About eighty years ago, the Dallas Park and Recreation Board purchased two dozen miscellaneous animals from the State Fair of Texas. In the ensuing years the **DALLAS ZOO,** located on 50 beautifully-landscaped acres in Marsalis Park just south of downtown Dallas, has increased its population to more than 2,000 animals representing 600 species.

The Dallas Zoo, aided by the support of the Dallas Zoological Society, has been the recipient of national awards for its extraordinary achievements in the breeding of rare animals.

Pictured here is the beautiful Flamingo Pool displaying three of the world's six remaining species of flamingos in the largest flock exhibited in any U.S. zoo.

Other popular features include the Great Apes, the Big Cats, the Tropical Rainforest, and a special Children's Zoo. Children and adults alike will enjoy a tour of the park on the Scenic Railway.

International Wildlife Park, west of downtown near I-30 and Beltline Road, is a 350-acre drive-through park featuring one of the country's finest free-roaming collections of exotic wildlife. Visitors can observe more than 2,000 animals in a natural habitat as they drive through the park in the safety of their automobile.

The Dallas Museum of Natural History is located in Fair Park and displays 54 natural habitats authentically recreated and furnished with actual specimens of Texas animal and plant life, including a fossil fish 90 million years old!

Also located in Fair Park, *The Dallas Aquarium* exhibits 340 species of amphibians, reptiles, and fish.

The Master Plan for the **DALLAS ARBORETUM AND BOTANICAL GARDENS** is another prime example of the "Dallas way" of doing things. This $50 million ten-year master plan was developed by internationally-recognized landscape architects, Jones and Jones, of Seattle, Washington, for the Dallas Arboretum and Botanical Society.

Located on 66 beautiful acres bordering White Rock Lake in east Dallas, this splendid facility will include a variety of specially-designed gardens, botanical exhibits, educational and research facilities, a lakeside amphitheatre, and a 300-seat garden restaurant.

The Dallas Civic Garden Center has been educating the public in the botanical sciences since 1936 with a wide variety of courses ranging from seed planting to tree maintenance.

More than 5,000 species of plant life have been grown in the seven-acre garden located within Fair Park. Each year more than 6,000 Dallasites enroll in Garden Center classes conducted in the center's 7,000-square-foot conservatory. The 600-seat auditorium is the site of frequent special events, seminars, and lectures; and the unique Tropical Garden Room, with waterfall and pool, houses a wide variety of tropical and aquatic plants.

Since the opening of **SIX FLAGS OVER TEXAS** in 1961, more than 50 million guests from around the world have experienced the thrills of the park's 205 acres of rides and attractions.

Pictured here is the $4.2 million Roaring Rapids river ride which simulates the experience of running the rapids in a raft. Other popular rides include the Cliffhanger which provides a 9-story free-fall experience; the Texas Shootout, a 200-foot parachute drop; and the world's largest and fastest double-loop roller coaster.

The park also features daily full-scale musical productions, and frequent appearances by popular entertainers at the 5,000-seat Music Mill amphitheater.

Six Flags is one of the finest entertainment values available in the Dallas area. Plan on spending an entire day at the park if you hope to see it all, and by all means, wear your most comfortable shoes!

While in the Six Flags area, you should plan to visit the *Wax Museum of the Southwest,* and the *Texas Sports Hall of Fame.*

The Wax Museum, largest of its kind in the Southwest, features 180 famous personalities recreated in 80 wax scenes.

The nearby Texas Sports Hall of Fame is a $4.5 million, 29,000-square-foot tribute to outstanding sports heroes, featuring an impressive collection of sports memorabilia, and several high-tech computerized exhibits.

If Dallas summers are too hot for you, cool off in style at **WHITE WATER.** This multi-million dollar 27-acre water park is the perfect place to beat the Texas heat.

Pictured above are two of the park's 12 major attractions. The Bermuda Triangle, with its three twisting and turning 60' water slides, is one of the most popular rides; and the Great Sea Wave, a pool the size of a football field, produces waves that simulate an ocean beach environment. Another favorite is the 275' water slide appropriately called White Lightning.

The price of admission gives you unlimited access to all rides, and whether you're there to experience the thrills and excitement, or just to lie in the sun between occasional dips in the park's 2.5 million gallons of water, you'll have a great time at either of the two Dallas-areas White Water parks. Both parks are equipped with ample locker room facilities, as well as food and beverage concessions. Picnic tables and deck chairs are plentiful, and there are many conveniently located shaded lounging areas.

According to informed sources, the intended purpose of the hole in the roof of **TEXAS STADIUM** was to permit God an unobstructed view of his favorite football team! Yet there are probably legions of envious football fans across the nation who would even challenge the right of the **DALLAS COWBOYS** to claim the title of "America's Team".

But the facts are inescapable. Twenty-five years ago, Dallas sportsman and civic leader, Clint Murchison, Jr., sent his infant Dallas Cowboys, an NFL expansion team, onto the field for the first of eleven thrashings it would receive during its initial NFL season. It took 35-year-old rookie head coach Tom Landry just six seasons to establish a tradition in Dallas which has resulted in an NFL record 19 consecutive winning seasons.

Indeed Mr. Murchison had a unique plan for building a football dynasty in Dallas: hire a brilliant executive with a football background to manage the club; find a player scout with a real nose for talent and give him the tools to provide the Cowboys with star-quality players year after year; and bring in a bright and enthusiastic field general with a firm grip on fundamentals and a flair for the innovative — the kind of man whose leadership would inspire greatness and a winning tradition.

Then, when you've hired a Tex Schramm, a Gil Brandt, and a Tom Landry, you turn it over to them and stay out of their way for 25 years! The rest is football history.

In April of 1980, successful Dallas businessman, Don Carter, met with Norm Sonju and Doug Adkins at a north Dallas coffee shop to discuss their final offer following months of negotiations in connection with their determined effort to bring NBA basketball to Dallas. After working out the terms on a napkin, they forwarded their final offer to the NBA expansion committee. Two weeks later an NBA franchise was awarded to the **DALLAS MAVERICKS.**

Meanwhile, in downtown Dallas, a magnificent $27 million sports and entertainment facility, Reunion Arena, was opening its doors for the first time. Dallas, Texas had a new basketball team, and the Dallas Mavericks had a new home.

Within three months, pro basketball's third-winningest active coach, Dick Motta, was recruited to lead the Dallas Mavericks against such basketball legends as the Los Angeles Lakers, the Philadelphia 79ers, and the Boston Celtics.

Few would have believed then, that in just four NBA seasons, the heroic Dallas Mavericks, cheered on by thousands of wonderfully-fanatic fans, would battle their way into the NBA playoffs and challenge the great Los Angeles Lakers for the conference championship. Deja Vu? Can the miraculous Mavericks live up to the unparalleled winning tradition established by the Dallas Cowboys? Go for it, Mavs!

47

O.K. So you've read about the Cowboy football dynasty, and the Miracle Mavericks, and now you're thinking, "Oh yeah? So what about the **TEXAS RANGERS?**"

In defense of Dallas' winning tradition, let's hasten to point out that the Texas Rangers Baseball Club is not a Dallas-based operation (note the conspicuous absence of "Dallas" in the name); and the team is owned and controlled by a guy who lives in Ft. Worth!

In defense of the Rangers' disappointing performance since entering the American League in 1972, let it suffice to say that after years of seemingly endless trades and highly-publicized free agent deals, and after numerous changes in leadership at all levels, including a dozen managers in as many years, the Texas Rangers could hardly be expected to win consistently.

However, many loyal Metroplex baseball fans have kept the faith and been no less grateful for the opportunity to see the world's great baseball teams play in their hometown. Hopefully the Rangers' ownership will soon reward them with the kind of leadership and stability that it takes to field a winning team.

The recently expanded and modernized Arlington Stadium is an excellent place to watch major league baseball, and diehard baseball fans continue to support the Rangers, win or lose.

Among the 22,000 acres of parks maintained by the City of Dallas are several fine municipal golf courses, including the 36-hole Tenison Park facility in east Dallas, where golfing great, Lee Trevino, learned the game.

More than twenty private country clubs offer a wide variety of challenging courses, including the excellent facility located at the Las Colinas Sports Club which now hosts the annual **BYRON NELSON CLASSIC.**

The Nelson Classic has become one of the major events on the PGA tour since its inception in 1968, and each year's tournament provides Dallas-area golf fans with an entire week of social galas, exciting pro-ams, and three days of championship golf.

Credit for this first-class sports spectacular goes to the

Salesmanship Club of Dallas which has sponsored the event since 1968. The Salesmanship Club, a prestigious organization of civic-minded Dallas businessmen, has successfully met the needs of hundreds of youngsters who have found solutions to menacing emotional and behavioral problems while under the care and guidance of dedicated counselors at one of the Club's special camps. These camps are funded with the proceeds of Salesmanship Club-sponsored events such as the Nelson Classic.

After more than sixty years of community service, the Salesmanship Club of Dallas is a prime example of the kind of spirit and leadership that has made Dallas one of the world's great cities.

This unusual scene has been included to demonstrate that the City of Dallas is not governed by the narrow-minded stuffed-shirt type of leadership that is generally thought of as "the Establishment" by the younger generation.

After all, you would have to be pretty "cool" to let a bunch of Rock'n Rollers dump 50 tons of sand on the promenade in front of City Hall, chlorinate the fountain pool for swimming, bring in a half-dozen rock bands, and several beer trucks to stage a **DOWNTOWN BEACH PARTY** for the benefit of the Muscular Dystrophy Association!

Fortunately, the well-behaved crowd created no problems for the men in blue who were there to keep things under control, and by the following day there wasn't a trace of what will hopefully become a unique annual event in downtown Dallas. Thumbs up for the boys at City Hall for striking a blow at the generation gap!

Pictured here is a scene easily identified by at least 250 million television viewers in more than 85 countries all over the world. **SOUTHFORK RANCH** is the home of the world's favorite villain, J.R. Ewing, and his family.

Although J.R. is by no means typical of the many successful Dallas oilmen, the top-rated "Dallas" television series has made its namesake city a source of considerable fascination in just about every corner of the world.

Since the majority of loyal "Dallas" fans may never have the opportunity to visit this beautiful city, international distribution of this book hopefully provides many of them with a chance to take a close-up and exciting look at the real Dallas.

Texas, with its 6,300 square miles of **LAKES AND STREAMS,** is second only to Alaska when it comes to accommodating its fishermen and water sports enthusiasts.

Lake Ray Hubbard, a 22,745-acre reservoir located 10 miles east of Dallas, is owned by the City of Dallas and provides the city with its water supply. The surrounding area, accessed by Interstate 30, has been the site of considerable development during the past few years and many Dallasites are choosing to live near the lake and commute to the city daily. Lake Hubbard is well-suited to water sports, and it offers excellent fishing for the serious angler.

Three smaller lakes are located within the city. Scenic White Rock Lake in northeast Dallas is favored by sailboating enthusiasts, picnickers, and local fishermen. The perimeter drive is very popular for top-down cruising,

cycling on summer afternoons, and running events.

Bachman Lake, located in northwest Dallas near Love Field, has a paved pathway circling the lake, and is popular among outdoor roller skaters and joggers.

Mountain Creek Lake, pictured above during a beautiful Texas sunset, is a 2,940-acre lake located in southwest Dallas near the Dallas Naval Air Station; and it provides convenient fishing and boating facilities for local residents.

Within convenient driving distance of Dallas are many other major lakes, including the enormous 89,000-acre Lake Texoma on the Texas-Oklahoma border. Lake Texoma's 580-mile shoreline provides abundant marinas, resorts, and camping facilities, as well as some of the best fishing in the nation.

Need a place to park your horse? How about a 42-acre multi-million dollar hotel for horses?

The **LAS COLINAS EQUESTRIAN CENTER,** located in beautiful Las Colinas just west of downtown Dallas, is a world-class equestrian facility where magnificent hunting and jumping horses are boarded, groomed, and trained for Dallas-area horse enthusiasts.

The center's 434′X80′ stable features individual 12′X12′ stalls equipped with automatic watering, feeding, ventilating, and fly-spray systems. The covered arena is one of the southwest's largest, and it hosts the annual Mercedes Grandprix Series of Show Jumping. This 30-event national tour offers more than $1 million in prize money, and

consists of 30 events held under the auspices of the American Grandprix Association.

The center offers English riding classes for novice riders, and school horses are available for those who do not own a horse. Supervised training programs and expert hunter-jumper instruction prepares local riders for show jumping competition.

Other notable features of the center include a comfortable observation lounge overlooking the arena, and an excellent tack shop offering the finest in English-style riding equipment and clothing. Visitors are welcome at this impressive facility which is located on Royal Lane a few miles west of I-35.

These cowboys don't wear helmets. If they were worried about gettin' hurt, they'd be playin' football or hockey in a bunch of fancy pads instead of ridin' bulls and wild horses at the **MESQUITE CHAMPIONSHIP RODEO.**

And these particular cowboys ain't no ordinary cowboys. Between them, they've won more than a million dollars in prize money and ten world championship titles while competing with thousands of cowboys who ride in the 600 Professional Rodeo Cowboy Association-sanctioned rodeos all over the country.

Pictured here (l. to r.) are Don Gay, eight-time world champion bull rider; Pete Gay; and Monty Henson, three-time world champion saddle-bronc rider.

Any visitor to the Dallas area during the April to September rodeo season would be remiss indeed to leave without seeing at least one authentic action-packed Texas rodeo. Fact is, for visitors and locals alike, the Mesquite Rodeo is one of the most exciting and entertaining evenings that can be had in the Dallas area. It's family fun at its best, and the action will keep fans of all ages on the edge of their seats. Check out the rodeo on I-635 at the Military Parkway exit on the far eastern side of Dallas.

And while you're in the Mesquite area, don't overlook the *Mesquite Opry* where you'll find down-home country-style entertainment by the folks who invented it.

THE LONGHORN BALLROOM, originally built by Dallas developer, O.L. Nelms, for legendary country star Bob Wills, has been operated by Dewey Groom since 1958 and has provided Country & Western music fans with year-round star-quality entertainment.

The Longhorn is a favorite among conventioneers, tourists, and travelers who want to sample some real live country music, some authentic Western-style dancin', and enjoy the company of some genuine country folks. The Longhorn is located on the edge of downtown Dallas near the convention center, and is a must-see for Dallas-area visitors.

Those who want an even larger slice of Western-style living will enjoy a day or two at *Big D Ranch,* about a half-hour south of Dallas off of I-45. This 600-acre working cattle ranch offers a variety of amusements and activities including country dances, rodeos, horseback riding, and hay rides. Big D Ranch is the perfect place to get away and relax for a spell, and it's also a popular location for small conventions and weekend business retreats.

DALLAS NIGHTLIFE would be a fitting subject for an entire volume, and since there are a number of fine restaurant and entertainment guides available to Dallas residents and visitors, we will only touch on the subject briefly.

Though downtown entertainment opportunities are expanding at a rapid pace, particularly now that the arts district project is underway, the city lacks a large recognizable downtown entertainment district like those commonly found in major international cities.

Consequently, most of the action takes place in a number of suburban locales such as the legendary Greenville Avenue Strip which offers mile upon mile of restaurants, nightclubs, bars, and specialty shops.

Pictured here is *Cafe Dallas,* the flagship of the Greenville Avenue fleet. Here you'll find a warm, luxurious decor and lots of sharp-looking young professionals who can tell you all about life in "Big D". The "born to party" crowd will enjoy nearby *Confetti,* a pull-out-the-stops and get-crazy kind of place. Further north on the strip, nostalgia buffs will find *Studebakers* which features 50's and 60's music and decor; and just around the corner, you'll find one of Dallas' most popular nightspots, *In Cahoots.*

Even those who live in Dallas would be hard-pressed to keep up with the entertainment opportunities offered throughout the city, so visitors should consult the guides and follow their instincts.

Whether you're a sophisticated gourmet in search of the perfect dining experience or a hungry tourist on a limited budget, you'll find **DINING IN DALLAS** can be rewarding and satisfying.

We couldn't begin to describe the wide variety of cuisine available or the multitude of dining establishments in the Metroplex; but fortunately there are several good restaurant guides available in the Dallas area for those who would like to review the options.

The weekend entertainment guides of both Dallas newspapers, published in the Friday editions, offer a useful listing of many of the city's more popular restaurants and cafes; but the most comprehensive listing may be found in *D Magazine*. "D" describes, reviews, and rates more than 250 restaurants throughout the Metroplex. Business hours, price range, and credit card information is included, so regardless of your tastes or budget, you'll find several great places to eat in "Big D".

The elegant scene pictured here is the beautiful La Champagne Restaurant in the Registry Hotel.

Baylor University Medical Center has been a leader in many areas of medical research, including the applications of nuclear technology in the diagnosis and treatment of disease.

Amber University, a fully-accredited institution, offers a variety of undergraduate and graduate degree programs with curricula and schedules specifically tailored to the needs of working adults as well as full-time students.

Education, Religion, & Health

First Baptist Church, located in downtown Dallas, is the largest Baptist church in the world with a total membership of 25,000.

Education is a high priority in Dallas. The city's 20 public high schools are augmented by six magnet high schools offering specialized career training in a variety of fields, including business, health, transportation, human services, and the arts.

In 1970, the Dallas Independent School District opened Skyline Career Development Center, a $21 million education complex which includes a comprehensive high school, a career development center offering advanced vocational training, and a community service center providing a source of continuing education for Dallas residents.

Higher education opportunities are abundant in the Dallas area with twenty-six 4-year degree-granting institutions and nineteen 2-year degree-granting colleges within a 100-mile radius.

SOUTHERN METHODIST UNIVERSITY, located on a 164-acre campus in University Park, five miles north of downtown Dallas, offers degree programs in sixty major fields. This beautiful campus serves more than 9,000 students, including graduates, and about half of the undergraduate students live on the campus.

Among SMU's outstanding graduate programs are its School of Law and the many business-related graduate degrees offered by the Cox School of Business. Many of Dallas' top business and civic leaders were educated at SMU, and it continues to be a source of quality leadership for the rapidly-expanding business community.

The **UNIVERSITY OF DALLAS,** a private school affiliated with the Roman Catholic Church, is located on a 1,000-acre suburban campus in Irving, a few miles northwest of downtown Dallas.

Degrees are offered in art, biology, chemistry, biochemistry, classics, drama, economics, education, English, foreign languages, history, mathematics, philosophy, physics, politics, psychology, and theology.

Pre-professional programs are offered in architecture, business management, dentistry, engineering, law, and medicine; and the graduate school offers several advanced degrees including a 5-year MBA program.

More than half of the undergraduates are from out-of-state, and 70 percent of the student body live on the beautiful spacious campus which serves a total enrollment of about 3,000 students.

The Baptist General Convention of Texas also supports an institution of higher learning in the Dallas area. *Dallas Baptist College* is located on a 200-acre suburban campus 13 miles from downtown Dallas, and provides its 1,500 students a quality education in a religious atmosphere.

The college offers 33 major fields and four pre-professional programs through its schools of Arts & Sciences, Management & Free Enterprise, Education & Learning Resources, Nursing & Health Sciences, and Christian Faith & Learning.

The high priority placed on public education in Dallas is further evidenced by the excellent **DALLAS COMMUNITY COLLEGE SYSTEM** with seven beautiful campuses throughout Dallas County.

Once again, Dallas' visionary civic leaders saw a need and developed an ambitious master plan for a seven campus system of 2-year community colleges that could serve an enrollment of 75,000 students by the year 2000. Dallas voters said Yes, and 41.5 million 1965 dollars were devoted to launching the Dallas County Community College District.

Soon the system's seven individually-designed and landscaped campuses were offering Dallas County residents a vast array of credit and non-credit courses of every category and description. By 1981, 19 years ahead of original projections, the DCCCD had a combined student body of 75,000 students.

In 1961, just a few years prior to the establishment of the DCCCD, another group of concerned civic and industrial leaders took the initiative and began to develop plans for a Graduate Research Center to attract top echelon scientific minds and research programs to the Dallas area.

The Southwest Center for Advanced Studies, as it was later named, was destined to become an internationally-recognized graduate education and research facility.

Thus, in the Fall of 1969, **THE UNIVERSITY OF TEXAS AT DALLAS,** opened its doors to a small group of graduate students in mathematics and natural science.

By 1983, UTD's enrollment, which is restricted to graduates and upper-division undergraduates, had grown to more than 7,500 students pursuing 59 degree programs, including master's degrees in 19 fields, and Ph.D's in 11.

The modern $90 million campus, located in the suburban city of Richardson, covers 500 acres and includes 14 major structures.

UTD's research staff consistently ranks among the state's top three in research funding per full-time faculty member; and its programs in Interdisciplinary Studies permit many successful Dallas professionals an opportunity to enhance their academic credentials with flexible degree plans.

Among the many important scientific projects underway at UTD as of this writing, is the development of computer programming that will operate all systems of a multi-national space mission to intercept and study Haley's Comet for evidence of its origin and composition.

Ms. Lillian Bradshaw, director of the Dallas Public Library System, says, "The new Central **DALLAS PUBLIC LIBRARY** is the world's best library — technologically and architecturally".

Once again, the City of Dallas has spared no expense in providing its citizenry with a new 636,733 square foot, ten-level downtown library. This state-of-the-art, fully-computerized central library was completed in 1982 at a cost of $42.7 million, and it has an expandable capacity of 2.3 million volumes with seating for 3,000 patrons!

The central library is augmented by 17 branch libraries located throughout the city, and together they provide Dallas residents with the fourth largest circulating library among the nation's ten largest cities.

Among the new library's many special features are several private study areas, a cable television studio, a listening center for recordings, a darkroom, microfilm and videotape viewing facilities, a completely computerized cataloging system with more than 80 terminals for convenient use, and access to more than 200 data bases for comprehensive research in the areas of science, business, education, humanities, and social sciences. The building also contains a spacious exhibit hall and a 200-seat auditorium.

Strong religious influences are present at all levels of Dallas' civic and business leadership; and as a result, the city benefits from a wide variety of thriving church congregations and Christian social ministries which serve the community's spiritual, emotional, and physical needs.

Nearly all denominations are represented among the 1,200 churches and synagogues located in Dallas, and some of the nation's largest church congregations are located here.

Beautiful Highland Park Methodist Church, pictured here, is but one example of the many inspirational worship facilities available to Dallas residents.

The Greater Dallas **COMMUNITY OF CHURCHES** plays an important role in coordinating the efforts of the many denominations which share a common interest in ministering to the spiritual needs of Dallas' rapidly-expanding population. Numerous other interfaith ministerial associations are instrumental in the development of a wholesome moral climate in this city.

Of particular interest to visitors and residents in the Dallas area is the unique *Biblical Arts Center* located in north Dallas near Northpark Mall. This center features early-Christian architecture, a biblical and secular art collection, and a magnificent 120' X 20' oil painting of the Miracle at Pentecost.

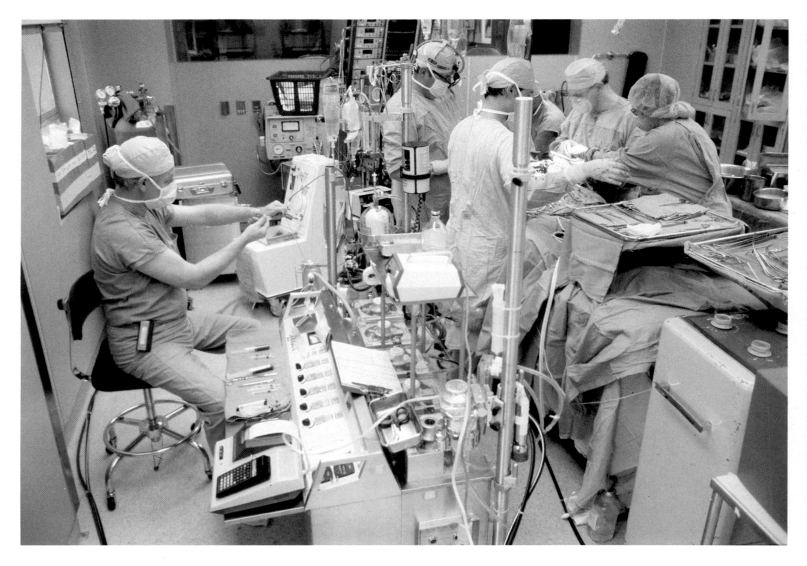

Medical facilities in Dallas are among the nation's finest, and they include two major educational and research institutions, ten nursing schools, and numerous allied health programs. A total of 10,710 hospital beds are available in Dallas County at present with several expansions underway.

BAYLOR UNIVERSITY MEDICAL CENTER was founded in 1903 and has since become the sixth largest general private hospital in the U.S., with 1,275 beds, about 900 staff physicians, and nearly 5,000 employees.

This 27-acre medical complex houses five hospitals for patient care, a teaching and research hospital, special centers for the diagnosis and treatment of heart disease and cancer, blood and plasma research facilities, and one of the country's most advanced Special Care Nurseries for the care of premature and critically-ill infants.

Also located at Baylor Medical Center are the Baylor University School of Nursing, and the Baylor College of Dentistry.

Though patient care is the primary mission of Baylor University Medical Center, its continued leadership in the development of new diagnostic procedures, specialized treatment programs, and advanced medical technology has brought international recognition to this outstanding medical complex.

Parkland Memorial Hospital, operated by the Dallas County Hospital District, was the first hospital in Texas to be certified as a Level 1 Trauma Center by the Texas Department of Health. Nearly 500 patients per day visit the Parkland emergency room, and more than 75% of the hospital's in-patient admissions are through the emergency room.

Parkland's 750-bed hospital admits more than 35,000 patients annually on a budget exceeding $123 million. This important teaching hospital's staff physicians number more than 500; and augmented by the distinguished faculty of the **UNIVERSITY OF TEXAS HEALTH SCIENCE CENTER,**

this sprawling medical complex provides almost 1,000 student physicians and nurses with comprehensive training and valuable experience in one of the state's busiest hospitals.

Parkland Hospital and the UT Health Science Center have combined their resources to provide a number of highly-specialized treatment facilities including the famous UT-Parkland Burn Center, a new Pediatric Trauma Center, a Cutaneous Medicine Center, and continued leadership in the advanced technologies related to the diagnosis and treatment of heart disease.

Highland Park Village, Dallas' and
America's first shopping center, opened for
business in 1931.

Shopping in Dallas

The city's newest shopping mall, The
Galleria, opened for business in
the fall of 1982.

For many years, **NORTHPARK MALL** was the flagship of Dallas shopping malls, and it remains the favorite of thousands of discriminating shoppers in the North Dallas area.

Located at the intersection of Central Expressway and Loop 12, this sprawling facility contains more than 125 retail stores, including Neiman-Marcus, Lord & Taylor, Joske's, and J.C. Penney.

Northpark is also the home of the Dallas Repertory Theatre, and one of the finest movie theaters in the city. The fully-enclosed air-conditioned mall has a cafeteria, several restaurants, and is also convenient to the wide variety of dining and entertainment opportunities offered on nearby Greenville Avenue.

PRESTONWOOD TOWN CENTER, located at Dallas Parkway and Beltline in the Far North Dallas area, was built in 1979 to serve the rapidly-increasing population of the North Dallas Corridor, and more particularly, the suburban city of Addison, which has been the sight of phenomenal commercial development during the past ten years.

This 92-acre development contains 1.2 million square feet of commercial lease space occupied by more than 170 retail merchants. Among these are several major department stores such as Neiman-Marcus, Lord & Taylor, Joske's, and J.C. Penney.

Year-round ice-skating can be enjoyed at the Ice Capades Chalet, located inside the mall; and fourteen movie screens are within a block of this modern fully-enclosed two-level shopping center.

A large percentage of new Dallas-area residents have found the suburban city of Plano to be an ideal place to make their new home and raise a family. Located in the northernmost reaches of the rapidly-developing North Dallas Corridor, Plano offers a wide variety and extensive selection of quality housing, and an excellent public school system.

COLLIN CREEK MALL, a 92-acre development with over a million square feet of retail lease space, provides first-class shopping facilities for Plano and Far North Dallas-area residents. This 162-store mall, completed in 1981, includes five major department stores: Lord & Taylor, Dillards, Sanger-Harris, Sears, and J.C. Penney.

Collin Creek Mall also features a first-run movie theater, and a unique creekside Village Walk where a wide variety of handcrafted products are offered.

The futuristic design of **TOWN EAST MALL** is a familiar landmark on I-635 in far East Dallas County. This 1.1 million square foot facility was opened in 1971 and is now occupied by more than 150 retail merchants.

Four major department store chains are represented at Town East Mall: Dillard's, Joske's, Sanger-Harris, and Sears. Two multi-screen movie theaters are located nearby, as well as a number of fine restaurants.

Located on I-635 between I-20 and I-30, this mall is convenient to the Pleasant Grove and White Rock areas of East Dallas, and the suburban cities of Garland and Mesquite.

VALLEY VIEW MALL, located in North Dallas on LBJ Freeway (I-635) at Preston Road, is currently Dallas' largest shopping center. More than 200 merchants occupy 1.5 million square feet of lease space.

The newly-remodeled and expanded mall also ranks first among Dallas shopping centers in total retail sales volume.

Valley View Mall features a broad assortment of specialty shops and four major department stores: Sanger-Harris, Dillard's, Sears, and a fabulous new Bloomingdale's store — the only one to be found west of Philadelphia.

A first-run motion picture theater and a large video arcade keep the kids entertained for hours while Mom and Dad enjoy the mall's unlimited choice of products and merchandise.

The city of Richardson, another North Dallas suburb, has shared in the phenomenal growth and prosperity of Dallas County. It is a major center for Dallas' growing high-tech industry, and it has long been recognized for its excellent public school system.

Located in Richardson at Beltline and Plano Road, **RICHARDSON SQUARE MALL** serves the shopping needs of Richardson and surrounding communities. The mall contains more than 110 stores which occupy almost a million square feet of lease space. Four major department stores are located at this fully-enclosed mall which was opened in 1977: Dillard's, Joske's, Sears, and Montgomery Ward.

In the suburban city of Irving, bordering Dallas on the west, shoppers prefer **IRVING MALL.** Located at Beltline and Highway 183, this 1.1 million square foot mall contains 140 stores includings Dillard's, Joske's, J.C. Penney, Mervyn's, and Sears.

Shoppers in the southwest reaches of Dallas County are served by **REDBIRD MALL.** This 1.2 million square foot mall is located at Camp Wisdom and U.S. 67; and its 135 stores include Joske's, J.C. Penney, Sanger-Harris, and Sears.

THE GALLERIA, located at the intersection of Dallas Parkway and I-635 in far North Dallas, is a major mixed-use development which opened for business in the fall of 1982.

The Galleria has a half-million square feet of office space, a beautiful 450-room **WESTIN HOTEL,** and a million square feet of retail shopping. The mall also features an indoor ice rink and a wide variety of entertainment and dining options.

Three exclusive national department store chains have facilities in the Galleria: Saks Fifth Avenue operates a 3-level, 120,000 square foot store; Marshall Field & Co. has a 3-level, 200,000 square foot store; and Macy's has opened a beautiful new 250,000 square foot store.

Easy access and free parking for 6,000 cars make the Galleria's many exclusive specialty stores and shops a convenient source for the very latest in fashion and quality merchandise.

Conveniently situated in downtown Dallas, the 5.5 acre **PLAZA OF THE AMERICAS** complex offers an exciting array of major retail merchants, unique specialty shops, luxury office space, restaurants, and a millpond ice skating rink in a 15-story glass-enclosed atrium.

At the heart of this magnificent development is the internationally-acclaimed **PLAZA OF THE AMERICAS HOTEL.** The tradition of excellence established by its London-based management company, Trusthouse Forte, is evident at every turn in this world-class 442-room hotel.

Award-winning restaurant, Cafe Royal, holds the exclusive Cartier "Elegance in Dining Award" for its fabulous atmosphere and French *nouvelle cuisine.*

Le Relais, a full-service restaurant, also offers an excellent menu in a setting reminiscent of a Parisian sidewalk cafe.

The Passerelle Bar spans the atrium above the ice rink affording its patrons a panoramic view of the entire complex; and the Lobby Bar provides piano music in an elegant, relaxing atmosphere.

An international multi-lingual executive staff provides reassuring personal service for foreign guests; and all hotel patrons will enjoy the first-class sports and recreational facilities of the Plaza Athletic Club.

First Class Hotels

"One measure of a city's hospitality is the manner in which it accommodates its visitors"

In 1912, the wealthy Missouri beer baron, Adolphus Busch, honored his beloved adopted hometown of Dallas with a beautiful new 21-story hotel. An original Dallas landmark, the **ADOLPHUS HOTEL** achieved world-class status with the recent completion of a $45 million renovation.

This historic 437-room facility offers 31 different room formats featuring exquisite Queen Anne and Chippendale decor; and the Grand Lobby, a portion of which is pictured above, is exceptionally elegant.

Conveniently located in downtown Dallas, the Adolphus takes great pride in its internationally-acclaimed French Room, which offers the world's finest *haute cuisine* in breathtaking regal surroundings.

The Grille offers breakfast, lunch, and dinner in a posh and private English setting; and the Palm Bar offers a lively and comfortable atmosphere for a tasty lunch, or a relaxing drink and conversation.

Service is impeccable at the Adolphus, as one would expect from a hotel with a 70-year tradition of excellence. The continental character of this fine hotel is evident from the moment the smartly-uniformed doorman bids you welcome; and upon entering, the senses are overwhelmed with suberb *objets d'art* throughout the spacious, opulent Grand Lobby.

The history and tradition of the Adolphus provide this modern space-age city with a living link to its rich heritage, providing a foundation for the kind of civic pride that has made Dallas one of the world's great cities.

Dinner in the exotic Pyramid Room, pictured here, is but one of the many memorable experiences that guests of the **FAIRMONT HOTEL** will enjoy. This internationally-acclaimed downtown hotel contains 600 guest rooms and 50 suites in its twin high-rise towers.

The Fairmont's tradition of excellence began in 1969, and within a few years it would become the standard to which Dallas hotels were compared.

Indeed, the Fairmont is the first hotel in the United States to hold three of the hotel industry's most prestigious awards — the Mobil Five Star Award, the AAA Five Diamond Award, and the Travel/Holiday Guide to Fine Dining Award.

Two ballrooms and 24 meeting rooms provide 65,000 square feet of meeting space; and the Brasserie Restaurant is open 24 hours a day for the convenience of Fairmont guests.

In addition to the outstanding *haute cuisine* of the Pyramid Room, Fairmont patrons enjoy an excellent menu in the Venetian Room, an intimate supper club that features the nation's top entertainers in an opulent 18th century decor.

For many years the Fairmont has been a favorite choice of those who demand fine atmosphere, service, cuisine, and entertainment.

A few years ago, Dallas commercial real estate developer, Trammell Crow, undertook the task of building a true world-class hotel on I-35 in the Dallas Market Center area. The Loews **ANATOLE HOTEL** was to be the flagship of Dallas hotels — an unsurpassed statement of luxury and design excellence with 900 guest rooms. At the hotel's dedication, a high-ranking Loews official said, "Only in Texas would we even attempt something like this."

Within months of its grand opening, the Anatole's spectacular twin atrium towers were operating at near capacity; and Mr. Crow soon unveiled an incredible $102 million expansion plan! By the end of 1983, the Anatole would be the largest, most complete, and most luxurious hotel and convention facility in Dallas.

This truly magnificent 41-acre complex, which includes seven acres of gardens and parks, contains 1,620 guest rooms; 145 suites; 19 restaurants and lounges offering award-winning cuisine and first class entertainment; 150,000 square feet of meeting and banquet space; six ballrooms, including a cavernous 30,000 square foot facility; six theater/lecture halls; 58 meeting rooms; and an incredible 72,000 square foot sports and recreation center!

Those who visit the Anatole and personally experience the magnitude and splendor of this one-of-a-kind facility, will leave with a new understanding of the ambition, talent, and courageous spirit that is characteristic of Dallas' leading developers.

The unique, dramatic design of the luxurious 1,000-room **HYATT REGENCY HOTEL,** and the adjacent 50-story *Reunion Tower,* are truly representative of Dallas today.

The incredible atrium lobby rises 200' above ground level, and contains a six-story vertical glass wall which overlooks the adjacent park and water garden. Inside and out, the Hyatt Regency provides an exciting visual experience that attracts visitors and guests from all over the world.

The Regency's specialty restaurant, Fausto's, features gourmet seafood delicacies, a piano bar, and a quiet, elegant dining area with a beautiful stained-glass decor.

The open-air coffee shop and sidewalk cafe, Cafe Esplanade, offers a wide variety of light entrees and an excellent view of the atrium area.

Park Place, the lobby bar, is the perfect place to relax and enjoy a cool drink and pleasant conversation.

Reunion Tower, soaring 600 feet above downtown Dallas, provides a breathtaking view of Dallas from its public observation deck. It also houses Antares, an elegantly-decorated restaurant serving a wide variety of luncheon and dinner specialties, and the Top of the Dome Lounge, featuring live entertainment nightly. Both the restaurant and lounge revolve slowly, affording guests a wonderful 360° view of the entire Metroplex.

The **DALLAS HILTON HOTEL,** located on Commerce Street in downtown Dallas, was opened in 1956, and now contains a total of 710 guest rooms and 30 suites.

Meeting and convention facilities include 37 meeting rooms, and a total of 14,445 square feet of ballroom space, including the 7,920-square-foot Grand Ballroom.

The hotel's first-class dining and entertainment facilities include: The Beef Baron, specializing in beef and seafood for lunch and dinner; El Cafetal, a convenient coffee shop in the main lobby area; the Library Lounge, ideal for refreshing drinks in a quiet, relaxed atmosphere; and the Gatsby's Bicycle Bar, a lively gathering place featuring excellent drinks and popular music.

It's difficult to describe the **MANSION ON TURTLE CREEK** because there is nothing that compares with it. Those who are willing to pay for the most exclusive accommodations in Dallas will love this intimate 143-room hotel in the beautiful Turtle Creek area, five minutes north of downtown Dallas.

This unusual hotel, built around the fabulous 60-year-old Sheppard King Mansion, was restored and expanded at a cost of $21 million in 1980. The traditional European decor is rich and elegant, and the atmosphere is quiet and private with an opulent residential ambiance.

The Mansion is regarded as a home-away-from-home by many famous celebrities who visit Dallas frequently. Each suite is individually and exquisitely decorated, and the hotel staff provides the kind of personal service that cannot be found in larger, more conventional hotels. The Mansion's expertly-managed staff actually maintains records of the personal preferences of their regular guests, such as favorite flowers, music, and culinary tastes, and prepares for their arrival accordingly.

For those who want privacy, personal service, and an elegant residential atmosphere, the Mansion is the finest Dallas can offer.

The beautiful 562-room **SHERATON PARK CENTRAL HOTEL** anchors the 1,878-acre Park Central complex in far North Dallas near the intersection of Central Expressway and I-635.

A spacious atrium lobby, with floors and walls of Italian Bottichino marble, creates an immediate impression of exceptional style and luxury.

The luxurious atmosphere is maintained throughout the hotel's custom-designed and furnished guest rooms, and its first-class dining and entertainment facilities are equally impressive.

Adjacent to the main lobby, a specialty restaurant, Mozart's, offers an atmosphere and menu reminiscent of early twentieth-century Vienna. Nearby, Cafe in the Park serves breakfast, lunch, or dinner in a charming Parisian sidewalk cafe setting. The Vienna Express provides a variety of tempting delicacies with quick service for those on the go.

Patrons who enjoy gourmet dining at its best will love the elegant surroundings and impeccable service at Laurels, a rooftop restaurant and lounge with a great view of the city.

After-dinner entertainment and dancing make for a lively evening at Covington's, and those who prefer a cool drink and conversation in a relaxing environment will enjoy the convenient Lobby Bar in the center of the atrium.

Pictured here in the foreground, adjacent to the Sheraton, is *Benihana's of Tokyo*. Benihana's provides excellent Japanese cuisine, and a unique oriental dining experience.

The **MANDALAY FOUR SEASONS HOTEL**'s wonderful accommodations and recreational facilities are so attractive that many of its regular guests are Dallas-area residents who check-in to this resort-type hotel for a convenient weekend of sports, recreation, and relaxation.

This beautiful 27-story, 424-room hotel is situated on the shore of Lake Carolyn in the heart of the Las Colinas community, just west of downtown Dallas. D/FW Airport is just a few miles away, and Venetian-style water taxis are available to transport guests through the network of canals that flow through the Las Colinas business and shopping districts.

Dining and entertainment facilities include Cafe D'Or, overlooking the courtyard and lake, which features a comfortable atmosphere and a fine family-oriented menu;

Enjolie, a five-star French gourmet restaurant ranked among Dallas' finest; and Rhapsody, a top-rated nightspot featuring programmed and live music for dancing, a light evening menu, and an interesting mix of hotel guests and local residents.

The Mandalay's big drawing card is the Las Colinas Sports Club which provides hotel guests with the most modern and complete sports and recreation center in the Metroplex. Its features include: golf on a championship course; racquetball, squash, indoor and outdoor tennis; swimming; whirlpools; health club and restaurant; nautilus equipment; English or Western-style riding; and a unique preventive medicine clinic offering physical exams, diagnostic testing, and nutritional assessment.

Dallas North Tollway is a major traffic artery from downtown Dallas to the far north Dallas area bounded by LBJ Freeway on the south and the emerging suburban cities to the north. Situated at the intersection of these two major arteries is the **LINCOLN HOTEL**, the focal point of the enormous *Lincoln Center* commercial development.

This modern luxurious hotel's 514 guest rooms include 39 suites and 21 banquet and meeting rooms, including a 10,000-square-foot ballroom.

Among this new hotel's many impressive features is Gallé Cuisine Continentale, with its art deco decor and outstanding international cuisine; and the Spinnaker Seafood Restaurant and Oyster Bar, offering expertly-prepared fresh seafood and an authentic seaside decor.

Other dining and entertainment facilities include an intimate Lobby Lounge; The Terrace Cafe situated in the beautiful open-air atrium, and Cricketeers, featuring daily luncheon specialties, more than three dozen imported and domestic beers, and nightly entertainment with live music and dancing.

The Lincoln is convenient to three of Dallas' largest and most popular shopping malls: the Galleria, Valley View Mall, and Prestonwood Town Center.

For your recreational pleasure, there are indoor and outdoor swimming pools, tennis courts, racquetball, indoor and outdoor jogging tracks, steam room, sauna, and whirlpool.

The Lincoln is one of several splendid Radisson Hotels and its first class facilities and service reflect the Radisson commitment to excellence, comfort, and convenience.

Located in Far North Dallas, near the intersection of Dallas Parkway and Beltline Road, the **REGISTRY HOTEL** provides first-class hotel accommodations for the rapidly-expanding commercial developments of the suburban city of Addison.

Addison Municipal Airport, one of the nation's leading private executive airports, is just five minutes away and both D/FW Airport and Dallas Love Field are within twenty minutes of The Registry.

You'll be immediately impressed with the five-story glass and marble atrium where the Garden Court Lounge is situated; and the elegant French dining room, La Champagne, offers excellent French cuisine.

Other dining and entertainment facilities in the 570-room hotel include Stetson's, offering Texas-style broiled steaks and one of Dallas' most extensive fresh seafood menus; Cafe Chablis, a 24-hour cafe with charming French decor; the Malachite Showroom, a 700-seat nightclub that showcases the finest entertainment this side of Las Vegas; and Ravel's, a popular nightclub frequented by many who live and work in the Addison area.

The hotel has excellent convention and meeting facilities, including the 25,000 square foot Crystal Ballroom; and two major shopping centers, containing more than 300 specialty shops and department stores, are within walking distance.

Recreational opportunities include both indoor and outdoor swimming pools, a health club, four tennis courts, two racquetball courts, and nearby golf courses.

The 21-story tower of the **DOUBLETREE HOTEL** is flanked by the twin towers of Campbell Center, an architectural landmark made famous by the familiar opening sequence of the "Dallas" television series.

The Doubletree shares the intersection of Central Expressway and Loop 12 with Northpark Mall and Northpark East. It is bounded on the east by Greenville Avenue, the site of dozens of Dallas' best restaurants and nightclubs.

The Doubletree's facilities include 302 deluxe guest rooms, more than 8,000 square feet of meeting space, and a 6,787-square-foot ballroom. Also available are 19 first-class suites, and 3 executive boardrooms with a beautiful view of the Dallas skyline.

The Princeton Grill offers an excellent menu with several unique house specialties; and the Cirrus Lounge, high atop the tower, offers live music, dancing, and a great view of the city in a comfortable, relaxing atmosphere.

Located in the ultra-modern Quorum commercial development on Dallas Parkway near Beltline Road in Far North Dallas, the beautiful **QUORUM MARRIOTT HOTEL** provides convenient access to the outstanding dining, entertainment, and shopping facilities in and around the city of Addison.

This 550-room hotel offers a warm and luxurious decor and all the comfort and conveniences upon which the Marriott chain has built its reputation.

Rambutan's provides Marriott guests with exquisite Chinese cuisine in an elegant Asian setting; and Chicory's Restaurant offers a delicious variety of selections for breakfast, lunch, or a full-course dinner.

Chicory's Lounge, a fashionable nightspot which is also popular among local residents, features live entertainment nightly, dancing, and a lively happy-hour crowd. The comfortable Lobby Bar has a quieter, more relaxed atmosphere for a casual drink and conversation.

Guests will enjoy both indoor and outdoor swimming pools, sauna, whirlpool, and exercise room; and fourteen movie screens are within a few blocks of the hotel.

The extraordinary **WYNDHAM HOTEL** is located in the heart of the Dallas Market Center on I-35 just ten minutes from downtown Dallas.

This impressive landmark, constructed entirely of Texas pink granite, offers 542 first-class guest rooms; meeting space for up to 600 persons; an elegant ballroom; the top-rated Bay Tree Restaurant for formal dining; The Cafe, open 24 hours; and the convenience of 24-hour room service.

Regardless of one's mood or preference, the Wyndham's four lounges offer the perfect environment for entertaining and relaxation.

The Lobby Bar provides a lively gathering place for guests and visitors. Those who prefer a more subdued atmosphere will enjoy the more intimate Buyers Bar, or the rich wood-panelled Library Bar. The Lounge features a grand piano and a large-screen television for group viewing.

Thirty stories above ground level, the Wyndham's rooftop Athletic Club offers guests a wonderful view of Dallas while enjoying the benefits of a large swimming pool, sauna, whirlpool, and exercise equipment; and the Pool Bar provides convenient refreshment.

Epilogue

If you have read the entire narrative that accompanies this pictorial essay, you should have a good grasp of Dallas today. Though there is much more that could be said about this remarkable city on the Trinity River, and though there are a great many unmentioned Dallasites who are worthy of recognition for their contribution to the city, this general overview is indicative of the character and spirit of what may be described as the nation's most dynamic city.

Where do we go from here? We think that Dallas is destined for even greater prosperity, and its continued growth is virtually assured due to its vast financial resources and talented aggressive leadership.

Perhaps the most important development in recent years has been the emergence of a new priority — cultural growth. This element represents the city's greatest challenge in its bid to achieve cultural recognition throughout the world.

Billions of dollars are being spent on the construction of world-class facilities for the advancement of the arts. As these facilities become available, equal zeal must be devoted to the discovery and support of artists of all types. Indeed, Dallas' $2.6 billion Arts District will be of little use without talented and prolific artists to bring it to life.

Many promising young artists have been forced by lack of sufficient financial resources to abandon, or at best postpone, their artistic goals in favor of simply earning a living. The centralization of the creative arts community is an important step toward nurturing the city's cultural growth. However, as long as developers and financiers are reluctant to provide affordable housing and work space for these artists, the Arts District will essentially be another impressive monument rather than a center for cultural education and development. All too often, developers are heard to say "we'd like to devote some of this downtown property to residential development, but it just isn't economically feasible," a euphemism for "there are more profitable uses for the land".

Admittedly, the profit motive is what Dallas was built on, and it remains the essence of free enterprise and economic growth. It must be understood, however, that the advancement and support of the arts cannot be secondary to the profit motive. There would scarcely be a single masterpiece on the wall at the beautiful new Dallas Museum of Art if the artists responsible for creating them had been forced to "show a profit". But, if the community will support their efforts and provide affordable accommodations for them, our artists will reward us with the only thing that can ultimately bring cultural recognition to Dallas — an outpouring of artistic achievement of international proportions.

There are other major developments that can have a dramatic impact on growth within Dallas rather than just outward expansion into the suburban areas. Public transportation is a vital element of inner city growth and cultural development. The recent establishment of the Dallas-Area Rapid Transit Board (DART) is indicative of the city's awareness of this high priority. No expense can be spared in providing the city with the finest and most efficient system of public transportation available.

The "Town Lake" project mentioned in the introduction is another visionary concept that can have an extraordinary impact on "life" in Downtown Dallas. Although the central business district provides many magnificent views of man's greatest architectural achievements, there is no significant retreat where downtowners can enjoy a refreshing change of scenery to a beautiful, "natural" environment. What could possibly add more beauty and character to Dallas' downtown than a beautiful recreational lake ringed by landscaped parks, marinas, and picturesque residential development? New York has Central Park, San Francisco has Golden Gate Park — and Dallas is debating its Town Lake.

As we approach the bottom line, we can only conclude that Dallas, Texas is indeed a city worthy of international recognition; and it continues to move in the right direction. Dallas' outstanding civic, business and cultural leaders will continue to meet the challenges of Dallas today.

PHOTOGRAPHY CREDITS